70 Promises of Jesus

The Power of the Gospel

Don Black

70 Promises of Jesus
Copyright © 2015 Donald Black

All rights reserved. No part of this book may be reproduced in any form or by any means, except for brief quotations in printed or online review, with the prior written permission of the publisher.

Published by CTVN Media, Wall PA

All Scripture quotations are taken from the New King James Copyright 1982 by Thomas Nelson, Inc. or New American Standard Copyright 1995 by the Lockman foundation.

Used by permission. All rights reserved.

ISBN: 978-0-9859384-5-1

Printed in USA

Dedication

This book sprung out of a time of need and disappointment. God met me in that dark hour with His Word of encouragement. I dedicate these pages to all those who are waiting patiently for their personal Word from God. I am so very grateful for His love, mercy, and faithfulness.

This book came to life suddenly and needed a lot of help to make it happen. I am thankful for my daughter Kelsy's creative design and quick work. Thank God for my wife Teri, Laurie Hamby, and Crystal Bynum for making the words, grammar, and sentences fit together. My heart is full of love and joy for each of our Cornerstone partners who share in this ministry and help take the Good News of the Kingdom to the world.

Don Black

Table of Contents

Preface 5

Introduction - Which Way To Turn 7

Chapter 1 - A Word From God 15

Chapter 2 - Stand on Your Word 27

Chapter 3 - Create a Promise Book 36

Chapter 4 - 70 Promises of Jesus 40

Chapter 5 - Your Promise Book................65

Preface

This is a book about promises. Webster defines a promise as "a statement telling someone that you will definitely do something or that something will definitely happen in the future."

We all make promises. Some we keep and some we forget. A promise creates a sense of excitement and hope, but it breaks our heart when they aren't kept. The Apostle Peter teaches that by the power that Jesus has already provided, we have everything we need to experience the abundant life He designed. He has made great and precious promises that we can be like Him. The sin, evil, and darkness of this world does not compare to the glory that we find hidden in Christ.

"Grace and peace be multiplied to you in the knowledge of God and of Jesus our Lord, as His divine power has given to us <u>all things</u> that pertain to <u>life and godliness</u>, through the <u>knowledge of Him</u> who called us by glory and virtue, by which have been given to us exceedingly <u>great and precious promises</u>, that through these you may be <u>partakers of the divine nature</u>, having escaped the corruption that is in the world through lust."

2 Peter 1:2-4 (NKJV)

<u>These are the promises of Jesus.</u>

<u>He will definitely keep them.</u>

<u>On that, you can place your trust.</u>

<u>They are guaranteed for eternity.</u>

Introduction

__Which Way To Turn?__

Serving in a ministry that broadcasts the Gospel is a wonderful blessing. I am very humbled to have been called by Jesus to join the work at Cornerstone. What Russ and Norma Bixler started more than 36 years ago has established a long legacy of obedience and sacrifice. God has used them and CTVN to literally touch millions of lives here in Western Pennsylvania and around the world. It is a privilege to be a part of Norma's team and to join with her, our board, our diligent staff, and our faithful partners. There is great joy in sharing ministry with such a God-honoring team of brothers and sisters.

Always, with the blessings come challenges.

This last year has particularly been very difficult. I believe that because Cornerstone has come so far and has done so much in obedience to God's call, the devil hates us. He hates you too. The enemy's plan is for us to stop broadcasting the Good News of the Kingdom. Demons and fallen angels look for areas to attack in order to hurt us or to at least slow us down. They work in this world to fight against God's truth and His Kingdom. This resistance comes in many forms: personal attacks by callers and in letters, other ministers who sometimes say hurtful things, equipment breakdowns that take us off the air, and an on-going attempt to obstruct or negatively impact the finances we need to grow the outreach. These are examples of some of the tangible issues, but there are others, such as sickness and accidents, that our staff and families experience which are meant to cause disappointment and sometimes even discouragement.

If you are a Christian who desires to walk in obedience to God's will, then I know that you too are facing these types of challenges.

You and I struggle with the same obstacles and adversity. It's a battle in a long-fought war that God wins.

> *"No temptation has overtaken you except such as is common to man; but God is faithful, who will not allow you to be tempted beyond what you are able, but with the temptation will also make the way of escape, that you may be able to bear it."*
> (I Corinthians 10:13)

Which path to follow?

Recently the ministry at Cornerstone was challenged by two different messages. Early one week, a brother in the Lord, who God has used before prophetically, sent our Board Chair and myself an email that contained a prophecy for CTVN. This word was a rather stern correction about the way we were seeking God and the operations of the ministry. Basically, the message was that we were not being spiritual enough.

I always take prophetic proclamations very seriously. The Bible instructs us to judge each prophecy by God's Word with confirmation from two or more other mature believers. But before we could take these steps, I received a second counsel from another person.

I had lunch with a pastor whom I greatly respect, and we focused our talk on ministry outreach. We had a great time of sharing, and as we started to wrap up to pay the bill and leave, we somehow got on the topic of the supernatural. He and I are in agreement that the gifts of the Spirit are still in operation today, but he offered me some leadership advice. He felt that some of Cornerstone's programming was too charismatic. He explained that when Christians tune in to watch one of our *Signs and Wonders* programs, they may change the channel because they don't agree. He suggested that we focus more on the evangelical messages of grace, love, and mercy. Basically, he was saying that we were too spiritual.

So within a matter of seven days, I received two separate messages: one, we were not spiritual enough, and the other, we were too spiritual. This really was confusing. I truly desire to be obedient to God, and here were two special brothers telling me two opposite things. Both of them were only motivated by a desire to help Cornerstone and me to follow God.

I went to the Lord in prayer with a simple question, "Father what are you saying?" I then called several of our board members for their wisdom. Cornerstone is blessed with a fantastic board of directors. These women and men are committed to God's work and to each other. We stand in ministry in unity and in commitment.

When I told them about the two different words, each basically said the same thing - that we should continue to pray and seek God together, and He would make the direction clear. So we decided to pray through the weekend and have a conference call together early the next week, after asking God for wisdom.

That Saturday night, Teri and I went to a special church service here in Pittsburgh. The speaker that evening ministers in the office of a prophet. His message was about the coming year of Jubilee and a special peace that God was bringing to His people. I enjoyed the teaching and felt God had brought Teri and me to the service to hear His Word about rest. But after he finished speaking, and as he started to minister to the church, he called Teri and me down to the front to receive a prophetic word.

God has given me prophetic messages before. They have always been encouraging, even when the word spoke of things that at the time I didn't understand. Paul taught that the gift of prophecy always builds up the hearer:

> *"But he who prophesies speaks edification and exhortation and comfort to men."*
> (1 Corinthians 14:3)

This prophecy was very powerful. The speaker didn't personally know us. God used him to minister to Teri and me in a mighty way. I will share this word with you a little later in the text.

I spent Sunday afternoon just resting and praying. In that season of prayer, the Holy Spirit spoke to me to "HOLD ON TO MY WORD." My mind immediately asked God …

Which Word am I to hold on to?

CHAPTER 1

A Word From God

Receiving a Word from God is a treasure and holds a powerful promise.

Then Jesus said to those Jews who believed Him, "If you abide in My word, you are My disciples indeed. And you shall know the truth, and the truth shall make you free" (John 8:31-32).

I want to be made free, and I know you do too. The first step Jesus taught in this scripture was to abide or dwell on His Word. After that, He promised we would understand the truth and find freedom.

At 3:00 A.M. the next morning, I sat up in bed wide-awake. The Spirit of the Lord reminded me that there are two primary sources for you and me to receive a Word from God:

1. The Bible
2. The Gifts of the Holy Spirit

The Bible is God's inspired Word. There are two Greek words that describe the way the Bible speaks to us.

The first is the word **logos**; λ'oγos *in the Greek means* "word," "reason," or "plan." In Greek philosophy and theology, *logos* meant the divine reason implicit in the cosmos, ordering it and giving it form and meaning.

The term *logos* means God's written Word.

The second term is the word **rhema**; ῥῆμα which literally means an "utterance" or "thing said" in Greek. It's a term that signifies the action of utterance.

A *rhema* equals God's revealed Word.

When we study the Bible, we are reading the *logos*, God's written Word. We renew our minds with the *logos*. When the Holy Spirit brings the logos to life for personal application, we are receiving a *rhema* from God.

For the word of God is living and powerful, and sharper than any two-edged sword, piercing even to the division of soul and spirit, and of joints and marrow, and is a discerner of the thoughts and intents of the heart (Hebrews 4:12).

How do we receive His *Rhema* Word?

The Gifts of the Spirit

But to each one of us grace was given according to the measure of Christ's gift. Therefore He says:

"When He ascended on high, He led captivity captive, And gave gifts to men" (Ephesians 4:7-8).

Have you ever questioned the purpose of the Gifts of the Spirit? How many are there? Why did God include them in

His design for us? He could hav
the angels do everything without
placing His Spirit in us. But that is not
what He desires. The will of the Father
is to bring us into an intimate
relationship with Himself.

Is the Holy Spirit an important part of your everyday life?

We need Him to be. The Holy Spirit
brings to us the supernatural ability to
be like Jesus. He is the conduit of God
who equips Christians to live the
abundant life Jesus promised. The fruit
of the Spirit (Galatians 5:22-23)
describe the temperament of our
Heavenly Father.

The gifts of the Spirit demonstrate the
ways of God to the world through the
Church.

of the scripture, I have had y-one gifts the Holy s. Most likely there are e not yet discovered; ays teaches us something new. The following overview will help you better understand just how much God loves us and what He has given us to impact our daily lives.

I have organized these gifts into three groups for study.

Group #1 - The corporate plan of God
Group #2 - His power
Group #3 - His nature and His ways

Group #1 - Leadership gifts that:
REVEAL and **DIRECT** the
CORPORATE PLAN of God

"And He gave some as apostles, and some as prophets, and some as evangelists, and some as pastors and teachers, for the equipping of the saints for the work of service, to the building up of the body of Christ; until we all attain to the unity of the faith, and of the knowledge of the Son of God, to a mature man, to the measure of the stature which belongs to the fullness of Christ. As a result, we are no longer to be children, tossed here and there by waves and carried about by every wind of doctrine, by the trickery of men, by craftiness in deceitful scheming; but speaking the truth in love, we are to grow up in all aspects into Him who is the head, even Christ, from whom the whole body, being fitted and held together by what every joint supplies, according to the proper

working of each individual part, causes the growth of the body for the building up of itself in love" (Ephesians 4:11-16 NASB).

These Church offices are commonly called the Five-Fold Ministry Gifts. They are put into place by God to build, unite, equip, and encourage Christians. Every fellowship should have these leadership offices/gifts in action:

1. Apostle
2. Prophet
3. Evangelist
4. Pastor
5. Teacher

Group #2 - Manifestation Gifts
that **REVEAL** the **POWER** of God

"There are varieties of effects, but the same God who works all things

in all persons. But to each one is given the manifestation of the Spirit for the common good. For to one is given the word of wisdom through the Spirit, and to another the word of knowledge according to the same Spirit; to another faith by the same Spirit, and to another gifts of healing by the one Spirit, and to another the effecting of miracles, and to another prophecy, and to another the distinguishing of spirits, to another various kinds of tongues, and to another the interpretation of tongues. But one and the same Spirit works all these things, distributing to each one individually just as He wills.
For even as the body is one and yet has many members, and all the members of the body, though they are many, are one body, so also is Christ. For by one Spirit we were

all baptized into one body, whether Jews or Greeks, whether slaves or free, and we were all made to drink of one Spirit. For the body is not one member, but many."

(1 Corinthians 12:6-14 NASB).

1. Word of Wisdom
2. Word of Knowledge
3. Faith
4. Gifts of Healing
5. Effecting of Miracles
6. Prophecy
7. Distinguishing of Spirits
8. Kinds of Tongues
9. Interpretation of Tongues

Group #3 - Motivational Gifts that **REVEAL** the **NATURE** and **WAYS** of God

"Since we have gifts that differ according to the grace given to

us, each of us is to exercise them accordingly: if prophecy, according to the proportion of his faith; if service, in his serving; or he who teaches, in his teaching; or he who exhorts, in his exhortation; he who gives, with liberality; he who leads, with diligence; he who shows mercy, with cheerfulness."

(Romans 12:6-8)

- Prophecy
- Service
- Teaching
- Exhorting
- Giving
- Leading
- Mercy

All of the five church leadership offices involve speaking God's anointed Word. When we are seeking His will, they are the first stop in the journey.

- Apostle
- Prophet
- Evangelist
- Pastor
- Teacher

Other gifted believers in the Body of Christ are also sources for receiving a *Rhema Word* from God. The Holy Spirit wants to use others to speak to you in these ways:

- Word of wisdom
- Word of knowledge
- Tongues
- Interpretation
- Encouragement
- Exhortation

CHAPTER

2

Stand on Your Word

When God gives you a *Rhema Word*, it is very important that you take steps to safeguard it and then implement it into your life. Remember that your enemy the devil wants to steal that Word from you. God gave it to you to encourage you and to help you take steps into victory. The devil doesn't want you to live victoriously; he wants you to be weak, confused, and defeated.

I told you earlier that God spoke to me on that Sunday afternoon to hold on to the Word He had given me. I then asked Him, "Which one?" At that point, the Spirit brought back to my memory Paul's warning to Timothy:

> *"But know this that in the last days perilous times will come. For men will be lovers of themselves, lovers of money, boasters, proud, blasphemers, disobedient to parents, unthankful, unholy, unloving, unforgiving, slanderers, without self-control, brutal, despisers of good, traitors, headstrong, haughty, lovers of pleasure rather than lovers of God, having a form of godliness but **denying its power**. And from such people turn away!"*
> (2 Timothy 3:1-5)

Paul was concerned about his adopted son in the faith who was serving in Ephesus as the pastor of the church. He describes the works of the flesh in the lives of people that Timothy was involved with in the ministry. He is spotlighting very evil actions that impacted the church. These acts were motivated by devils and demons. But in the middle of these difficult times, Paul is instructing Timothy to stand guard and not to deny the power of the Gospel.

God's Word to you is alive!

He showed me that the Bible is literally filled with thousands of promises. I know they are all for me, but how am I to know which ones are for right now? His answer was simple. The Holy Spirit will bring alive the promises for me to walk in today.

To get started, I decided to narrow down my list of promises to some of the ones that Jesus made in the Scripture. I started looking for them and found 70 promises in twenty-eight different categories. Those are the ones that I have focused on in this book. He also gave me a strategy of how to practically stand on these promises from Jesus.

Now we have started organizing our review of the promises that **Jesus** gave us, but what about the prophetic words **you** receive?

Prophetic Promises

Remember what Paul taught us in Hebrews:

> *"For the word of God is living and powerful, and sharper than any two-*

edged sword, piercing even to the division of soul and spirit, and of joints and marrow, and is a discerner of the thoughts and intents of the heart" (Hebrews 4:12).

Let's learn how to walk in the Spirit and be eager to receive a Word from Him. It is important to be in an environment where we can receive the prophetic Word of God. If we aren't, we will have limited ourselves to only the natural world, and God does all His work in the supernatural realm.

I began this book with a personal story of how, in a matter of seven days, I had received two different honest options regarding the ministry work at Cornerstone. Both were given by loving brothers whose only motivation was to be a blessing. One was basically stating that we were too spiritual, and the other saying that we were not spiritual enough.

Then Teri and I went to the special worship service where the speaker called us to the altar with a prophetic Word from God. I want to share that message with you now. My goal is not to impress you, but to glorify God for His clarification of what He intended for Cornerstone to do.

Prophecy given in the worship service:

"When we met yesterday, the Spirit of the Lord spoke to me very clearly about a changing dimension in your ministry that is coming this next year. The impact that you have now is regional, but God is expanding it to global."

"The first question that would come to mind is: 'Lord, how do you want me to do that?' God says, 'I have a plan that I am revealing to you very soon. I will open up significant opportunities.' And your desire to keep it spiritual is God's desire. Stay with that; keep it pure - and don't go back the other way, but introduce the gifts, ministries, etc., because God has given you an apostolic grace. There is authority on you. God is going to bring relationships to you with men that flow and function in that realm. You will start seeing a tremendous realm of influence. The program will be going in places that many TV ministries have not gone - to multiple languages, countries, and multiple cultures."

"God is going to bring you a team. The Lord says, 'You are not going to

have to do it alone; I will bring you a team.'"

To Teri: *"The Lord said that intercession is part of your grace and gifting. There is a prophetic anointing on you. Step into that anointing and intercession - praying - and God is preparing the foundations."*

"This next season will start out completely different. There will be continual shifting until you see the Holy Spirit break through in such a profound way."

"There will be resources that come from the North, South, East, and West. The Holy Spirit is getting ready to do something profound in this region. This area is going to become an epicenter of revival. The Bible says to shout it from the rooftops,

and that is part of your mission – to shout the gospel from the rooftops."

Prayer:

"Father, I pray that supernatural grace will flow through my brother and sister. Empower them today with wisdom, knowledge, and understanding. Cover those limbs that have no vitality in them. Release it from them. Put a supernatural covering over them. Send talent, talent, and more talent to them. Thank you for that, in Jesus' Name. Amen."

When we received this word, both Teri and I were speechless. God had answered the question once and for all. He is so kind to send to us His Word. It creates other questions, but I am confident that He will answer those when the time is right.

CHAPTER

3

Create A Promise Book

I have chosen 10 promises from the following list of 70 found in the NKJV translation of the Bible. These are the first wave that I am incorporating into my life. I have written them on 3x5 note cards and have them with me to memorize and meditate upon.

I have also handwritten this personal prophecy and a couple others in a personal journal. In it, I have also written my 10 personal promises from Jesus.

In this book, I have made a place for you to do the same. Pick your 10 promises and write them down beginning on page 36. Also write down any words God gives you as a prophecy or from your reading of the Bible and prayer time.

Expect to hear from Him. He really desires for your love relationship with Him to grow.

Fight the good fight.

Paul encouraged Timothy to use his *Rhema Word* as a weapon in the battle against the kingdom of darkness:

> *This charge I commit to you, son Timothy, according to the prophecies previously made concerning you, that by them you may wage the good warfare (1 Timothy 1:18).*

He also instructed the church at Ephesus to pick up the Word as a sword in this battle:

"And take the helmet of salvation, and the sword of the Spirit, which is the word of God" (Ephesians 6:17).

Let's get started.

I know that you will be blessed by just reading the following list of promises from our Savior and Messiah. They are all true, and my friend, they are all true for you today. Pick out 10 that the Holy Spirit uses to speak directly to your need. Write them in "Your Personal Promise Section" in Chapter 5 of this book. Also, say a special prayer to the Father, asking Him to speak to you and to lead you by the Holy Spirit.

Finally, record in this journal any *Rhema Word* that the Holy Spirit brings to your heart. They are precious promises for you to hold on to tightly. I am praying for you to not only hear His voice but also to joyfully obey it.

Our Heavenly Father has a very special plan for you that extends through the rest of this life and then continues into Jesus' 1000 Year Kingdom on earth. You have a big part to play in His Eternal Kingdom.

This is an exciting time to live! Let's spend every day walking on His path, empowered by the Holy Spirit to live out the abundant life that Jesus provided to each of us.

CHAPTER

4

70 Promises of Jesus

A Full and Victorious Life.

My Word ☐

1. *"The thief does not come except to steal, and to kill, and to destroy. I have come that they may have life, and that they may have it more abundantly."*
(John 10:10)

Your Emotional Needs:
Comfort.

My Word ☐

2. *"Blessed are those who mourn, For they shall be comforted."*
(Matthew 5:4)

Gift of Laughter.

My Word

3. *"Blessed are you who weep now, For you shall laugh."*
(Luke 6:21)

A Perfect Peace.

My Word

4. *"Peace I leave with you, My peace I give to you; not as the world gives do I give to you. Let not your heart be troubled, neither let it be afraid" (John 14:27).*

My Word

5. *"These things I have spoken to you, that in Me you may have peace. In the world you will have tribulation; but be of good cheer, I have overcome the world."*
(John 16:33)

You Will Receive Mercy.

My Word

6. *"Blessed are the merciful, For they shall obtain mercy" (Matt. 5:7).*

A Peaceful Rest.

My Word

7. *"Come to Me, all you who labor and are heavy laden, and I will give you rest. Take My yoke upon you and learn from Me, for I am gentle and lowly in heart, and you will find rest for your souls. For My yoke is easy and My burden is light" (Matthew 11:28-30).*

Your Physical Needs.

My Word

8. *"Blessed are you who hunger now, For you shall be filled." (Luke 6:21)*

My Word

9. *" Now if God so clothes the grass of the field, which today is, and tomorrow is thrown into the oven, will He not much more clothe you, O you of little faith?" (Matthew 6:30).*

My Word

10. *"But seek the kingdom of God, and all these things shall be added to you"* (Luke 12:31).

Rewards In This Life.

My Word

11. *"And everyone who has left houses or brothers or sisters or father or mother or wife or children or lands, for My name's sake, shall receive a hundredfold, and inherit everlasting life"* (Matthew 19:29).

My Word

12. *"who shall not receive a hundredfold now in this time— houses and brothers and sisters and mothers and children and lands, with persecutions—and in the age to come, eternal life."* (Mark 10:30)

My Word ☐

13. *"Assuredly, I say to you, there is no one who has left house or parents or brothers or wife or children, for the sake of the kingdom of God, who shall not receive many times more in this present time, and in the age to come eternal life"(Luke 18:29-30).*

My Word ☐

14. *"that your charitable deed may be in secret; and your Father who sees in secret will Himself reward you openly" (Matthew 6:4).*

My Word ☐

15. *" And whoever gives one of these little ones only a cup of cold water in the name of a disciple, assuredly, I say to you, he shall by no means lose his reward."*
(Matthew 10:42)

Answered Prayers.

My Word

16. *So Jesus answered and said to them, "Assuredly, I say to you, if you have faith and do not doubt, you will not only do what was done to the fig tree, but also if you say to this mountain, 'Be removed and be cast into the sea,' it will be done. And whatever things you ask in prayer, believing, you will receive" (Matthew 21:21-22).*

My Word

17. *"Again I say to you that if two of you agree on earth concerning anything that they ask, it will be done for them by My Father in heaven" (Matthew 18:19).*

My Word

18. *"Most assuredly, I say to you, he who believes in Me, the works that I do he will do also; and* *greater works than these he will do, because I go to My Father. And whatever you ask in My name, that I will do, that the Father may be glorified in the Son. If you ask anything in My name, I will do it" (John 14:12-14).*

My Word

19. "If you abide in Me, and My words abide in you, you will ask what you desire, and it shall be done for you" (John 15:7).

My Word

21. *"And in that day you will ask Me nothing. Most assuredly, I say to you, whatever you ask the Father in My name He will give you. Until now you have asked nothing in My name. Ask, and you will receive, that your joy may be full" (John 16:23-24).*

Being A Christian Isn't Easy.

My Word

22. "And you will be hated by all for My name's sake. But not a hair of your head shall be lost. By your patience possess your souls" *(Luke 21:17-19).*

Healing For Your Body.

My Word

23. *"For the hearts of this people have grown dull. Their ears are hard of hearing, And their eyes they have closed, Lest they should see with their eyes and hear with their ears, Lest they should understand with their hearts and turn, So that I should heal them."*
(Matthew 13:15)

My Word

24. *"But that you may know that the Son of Man has power on earth to forgive sins"— He said to the man who was paralyzed, "I say to you, arise, take up your bed, and go to your house" (Luke 5:24).*

You Have Divine Authority.

My Word

25. *"Because of your unbelief; for assuredly, I say to you, if you have faith as a mustard seed, you will say to this mountain, 'Move from here to there,' and it will move; and nothing will be impossible for you."*

(Matthew 17:20)

There Is Miraculous Power.

26. *Jesus said to him, "If you can believe, all things are possible to him who believes" (Mark 9:23).*

My Word

27. *"Assuredly, I say to you, whatever you bind on earth will be bound in heaven, and whatever you loose on earth will be loosed in heaven" (Matthew 18:18).*

My Word

28. Behold, I send the Promise of My Father upon you; but tarry in the city of Jerusalem until you are endued with power from on high."
(Luke 24:49)

My Word

29. *So Jesus answered and said to them, "Have faith in God. For assuredly, I say to you, whoever says to this mountain, 'Be removed and be cast into the sea,' and does not doubt in his heart, but believes that those things he says will be done, he will have whatever he says. Therefore I say* *to you, whatever things you ask when you pray, believe that you receive them, and you will have them" (Mark 11:22-24).*

My Word

30. *And He said to them, "Go into all the world and preach the gospel to every creature. He who believes and is baptized will be saved; but he who does not believe will be condemned. And these signs will follow those who believe: In My name they will cast out demons; they will speak with new tongues; they will take up serpents; and if they drink anything deadly, it will by no means hurt them; they will lay hands on the sick, and they will recover."*
(Mark 16:15-18)

My Word

31. *"Behold, I give you the authority to trample on serpents and scorpions, and over all the*

power of the enemy, and nothing shall by any means hurt you."
(Luke 10:19)

My Word

32. *But Jesus looked at them and said to them, "With men this is impossible, but with God all things are possible" (Matthew 19:26).*

God Will Honor You.

My Word

33. "If anyone serves Me, let him follow Me; and where I am, there My servant will be also. If anyone serves Me, him *My* Father will honor" (John 12:26).

The Power To Overcome.

My Word

34. *"for I will give you a mouth and wisdom which all your adversaries will not be able to contradict or resist" (Luke 21:15).*

My Word ☐

35. *"But when they deliver you up, do not worry about how or what you should speak. For it will be given to you in that hour what you should speak" (Matthew 10:19).*

My Word ☐

36. *"And I will give you the keys of the kingdom of heaven, and whatever you bind on earth will be bound in heaven, and whatever you loose on earth will be loosed in heaven" (Matthew 16:19).*

That You Can Be Free.

My Word ☐

37. *"If you abide in My word, you are My disciples indeed. And you shall know the truth, and the truth shall make you free."And you shall know the truth, and the truth shall make you free."*

(John 8:32).

38. *"Therefore if the Son makes you free, you shall be free indeed.*

(John 8:36).

You Can Be Saved.

39. *"For God so loved the world that He gave His only begotten Son, that whoever believes in Him should not perish but have everlasting life. For God did not send His Son into the world to condemn the world, but that the world through Him might be saved. He who believes in Him is not condemned; but he who does not believe is condemned already, because he has not believed in the name of the only begotten Son of God" (John 3:16-18).*

40. *"Also I say to you, whoever confesses Me before men, him the Son of Man also will confess before the angels of God. But he* *who denies Me before men will be denied before the angels of God" (Luke 12:8-9).*

My Word

41. *"For the Son of Man did not come to destroy men's lives but to save them…" (Luke 9:56).*

My Word

42. *"Behold, I stand at the door and knock. If anyone hears My voice and opens the door, I will come in to him and dine with him, and he with Me" (Revelation 3:20).*

Jesus will not reject you.

My Word

43. *"All that the Father gives Me will come to Me, and the one who comes to Me I will by no means cast out" (John 6:37).*

The Holy Spirit Will Help.

My Word

44. *"However, when He, the Spirit of truth, has come, He will guide you into all truth; for He will not* *speak on His own authority, but whatever He hears He will speak; and He will tell you things to come. He will glorify Me, for He will take of what is Mine and declare it to you. All things that the Father has are Mine. Therefore I said that He will take of Mine and declare it to you" (John 16:13-15).*

My Word ☐

45. *"For the Holy Spirit will teach you in that very hour what you ought to say" (Luke 12:12).*

My Word ☐

46. *"Behold, I send the Promise of My Father upon you; but tarry in the city of Jerusalem until you are endued with power from on high."*
(Luke 24:49)

My Word ☐

47. *"I am the vine, you are the branches. He who abides in Me, and I in him, bears much fruit; for without Me you can do nothing."*
(John 15:5)

My Word

48. *"At that day you will know that I am in My Father, and you in Me, and I in you" (John 14:20).*

My Word

49. And when He had said this, He breathed on them, and said to them, "Receive the Holy Spirit. If you forgive the sins of any, they are forgiven them; if you retain the sins of any, they are retained" (John 20:22-23).

My Word

50. *"I still have many things to say to you, but you cannot bear them now. However, when He, the Spirit of truth, has come, He will guide you into all truth; for He will not speak on His own authority, but whatever He hears He will speak; and He will tell you things to come."*

(John 16:12-13)

He Will Make It Clear.

My Word

51. *"He who has My commandments and keeps them, it is he who loves Me. And he who loves Me will be loved by My Father, and I will love him and manifest Myself to him."*
(John 14:21)

You Will Never Die.

My Word

52. *"nor can they die anymore, for they are equal to the angels and are sons of God, being sons of the resurrection" (Luke 20:36).*

The Devil Is Defeated.

My Word

53. *"And I also say to you that you are Peter, and on this rock I will build My church, and the gates of Hades shall not prevail against it."*
(Matthew 16:18)

You Will See God.

My Word

54. *"Blessed are the pure in heart, For they shall see God."*

(Matthew 5:8)

Rewards In Heaven.

My Word

55. *"Do you not say, 'There are still four months and then comes the harvest'? Behold, I say to you, lift up your eyes and look at the fields, for they are already white for harvest! And he who reaps receives wages, and gathers fruit for eternal life, that both he who sows and he who reaps may rejoice together" (John 4:35-36).*

My Word

56. *"Rejoice and be exceedingly glad, for great is your reward in heaven, for so they persecuted the prophets who were before you."*

(Matthew 5:12)

The Gift of Generosity.

My Word

57. *"But when you give a feast, invite the poor, the maimed, the lame, the blind. And you will be blessed, because they cannot repay you; for you shall be repaid at the resurrection of the just."*
(Luke 14:13-14)

My Word

58. *"Give, and it will be given to you: good measure, pressed down, shaken together, and running over will be put into your bosom. For with the same measure that you use, it will be measured back to you"* (Luke 6:38).

God Has A Kingdom.

My Word

59. *"Therefore whoever humbles himself as this little child is the greatest in the kingdom of heaven"* (Matthew 18:4).

The Teacher's Reward.

My Word

60. *"Whoever therefore breaks one of the least of these commandments, and teaches men so, shall be called least in the kingdom of heaven; but whoever does and teaches them, he shall be called great in the kingdom of heaven" (Matthew 5:19).*

My Word

61. *"Whoever receives this little child in My name receives Me; and whoever receives Me receives Him who sent Me. For he who is least among you all will be great."*
(Luke 9:48)

Power Of Forgiveness.

My Word

62. *"For if you forgive men their trespasses, your heavenly Father will also forgive you."*
(Matthew 6:14)

63. *"So My heavenly Father also will do to you if each of you, from his heart, does not forgive his brother his trespasses."*
(Matthew 18:35)

64. *"And whenever you stand praying, if you have anything against anyone, forgive him, that your Father in heaven may also forgive you your trespasses. But if you do not forgive, neither will your Father in heaven forgive your trespasses"* (Mark 11:25-26).

65. *"If you forgive the sins of any, they are forgiven them; if you retain the sins of any, they are retained"* (John 20:23).

The Power Of Persistence.

My Word

66. *"Ask, and it will be given to you; seek, and you will find; knock, and it will be opened to you. For everyone who asks receives, and he who seeks finds, and to him who knocks it will be opened. Or what man is there among you who, if his son asks for bread, will give him a stone? Or if he asks for a fish, will he give him a serpent? If you then, being evil, know how to give good gifts to your children, how much more will your Father who is in heaven give good things to those who ask Him!"*

(Matthew 7:7-11)

Jesus Is Coming Back For You!

My Word

67. *"Let not your heart be troubled; you believe in God, believe also in Me. In My Father's house are many mansions; if it were not so, I would have told you. I go to prepare a place for you. And if I go and prepare a place for you, I will come again and receive you to Myself; that where I am, there you may be also" (John 14:1-3).*

68. *Jesus answered and said to him, "If anyone loves Me, he will keep My word; and My Father will love him, and We will come to him and make Our home with him."*
(John 14:23)

Jesus Loves You.

My Word

69. *"As the Father loved Me, I also have loved you; abide in My love. If you keep My commandments, you will abide in My love, just as I have kept My Father's commandments and abide in His love. "These things I have spoken to you, that My joy may remain in you, and that your joy may be full" (John 15:9-11).*

The Good News will reach the entire world and then this age will end.

My Word

70. *"And this gospel of the kingdom will be preached in all the world as a witness to all the nations, and then the end will come" (Matthew 24:14).*

CHAPTER

5

<u>Your Promise Book</u>

It is very important to daily recharge your spirit and renew your mind with *God's Living Word*. Go back and read through the 70 promises that Jesus made in the Bible. Place a checkmark in the "My Word" box next to the ones that speak to you about where you are in life. Those are the promises to strongly hold on to. Below are ten spaces to write down your promises:

#1 Scripture

_____
_____
_____
_____
_____
_____
_____
_____

#2 Scripture

_____
_____
_____
_____
_____
_____
_____
_____

#3 Scripture

#4 Scripture

#5 Scripture

_____
_____
_____
_____
_____
_____
_____
_____

#6 Scripture

_____
_____
_____
_____
_____
_____
_____
_____

#7 Scripture

#8 Scripture

#9 Scripture

#10 Scripture

Hold On To Your *Rhema* Word.

It is also important to hold on to God's *Rhema Word* that He reveals to us in many ways. Sometimes it is in reading the Bible, in prayer or listening to music, or listening to a pastor, teacher, or prophet's message. Whenever you hear from God, write that Word down and hold on to it for strength, encouragement, and for power. Keep the promises you receive close to you and refer to them daily. Memorize your Words and use them to renew your mind.

Write your *Rhema* Words on the following pages and revisit them regularly. Don't allow your enemy to steal them from you.

God Gave This Word To Me:

The Good News Network!

Over forty-six years ago God birthed in the hearts of Norma and Russ Bixler the vision of Cornerstone Television. Then on Easter Sunday, April 15th, 1979, CTVN began broadcasting the Gospel!

Our mission continues to use media to share the Good News of Jesus with as many people as possible, as quickly as possible, in the power of the Holy Spirit all to the glory of God!

- Our goal is see millions worldwide saved and filled with the Holy Spirit.

- We are dedicated to the Great Commission, to go into all the world teaching, preaching, and demonstrating the love of God to make disciples and build the Church.

Join us and become a partner by calling (888) 665-4483 or visit www.ctvn.org.